Thanks, Elvis, for all the wonderful memories.

The Best of
Elvis
Collectibles

AUTHORS
Steve Templeton
Rosalind Cranor

CONTRIBUTING EDITORS
Ted Young
John Diesso

The Overmountain Press
JOHNSON CITY, TENNESSEE

The values in this book's price guide were attained by consulting with numerous collectors and dealers across the country, in order to give the Elvis fan and collector the most accurate values on each item.

However, the values in this guide do not set dealers' prices. Therefore, neither the publisher nor the authors will be responsible for any losses incurred by referring to this guide.

Additional copies may be ordered at
$19.95 each plus $2.00 postage and handling.
(Tennessee residents add 8¼% sales tax)

The Overmountain Press
P.O. Box 1261
Johnson City, TN 37605

Anyone who has questions regarding their collection may write to the publisher. Such inquiries will be passed on to the authors.

FIRST EDITION
A special limited edition was published simultaneously
— 200 numbered, hardcover, copies —
ISBN 0-932807-77-1

DEDICATION

This book is dedicated to Chucky.

ACKNOWLEDGMENTS

Without the help from the following people this book could not have become a reality:

Debi Butram

George DeYoung

Fred Whorbey

Gloria Richter

Pat Byers

David Newell

Linda Jones

Sylvia Martinez

Special Thanks:

Brian Clark — photography

Brynda Clark

Judy and Dennis Dans

Ed Strait

Photo Flash

A special appreciation is due to George Alvarez for his wonderful photography.

TRENDS

Following the death of Elvis Presley fifteen years ago, a frenzy of buying and selling took place among any and everyone, it seemed, who possessed an Elvis item.

Common in 1977 and '78 were the ads in daily newspapers and monthly magazines with people offering Elvis items for sale. The asking price for many of these items (which ranged from concert photos to cups that Elvis supposedly drank from) was little less than a king's ransom.

Further, the public was being bombarded with newly manufactured items, many of which were gaudy and embarrassing, to say the least. It seemed that any item bearing Elvis' name or likeness was being touted as a true collectors item.

Collector shows were also popping up. However, the shows in the late '70s seemed to be a marketplace for the vendor to hawk his wares and make a fast buck off an emotional fan.

Many people (including this author) thought all of the eccentric buying and selling was just a fad that would soon pass. Elvis was being promoted so commercially that it seemed the public would soon sicken with just the mention of his name.

However, what emerged through all of those commercial exploits is a genuine and authentic respect for one of the greatest legends in history. With the wonderful efforts by the Graceland organization, Graceland has been turned into one of the most popular sightseeing attractions in the country.

Along with this change is a truer and more knowledgeable understanding by the Elvis fan as to what the more desirable items in the field of collecting Elvis memorabilia really are. This knowledge can be attributed to many of the fine books that have been written about Elvis records and memorabilia. Hopefully, this book will be received and accepted in that category as well.

Another amazing phenomenon is the vast number of young people who have become Elvis fans and collectors. This is really astonishing, considering that many of these young fans were not born until after the death of Elvis Presley.

This accomplishment can be directly attributed to Elvis' undying charisma that still lives in his music and films. For even though Elvis was a giant among entertainers, he still maintained a genuine down-to-earth appeal that made his legions of fans feel as if he were the boy next door.

Let there be no mistake — the magic of Elvis Presley will live forever.

A BRIEF HISTORY OF
ELVIS PRESLEY ENTERPRISES

In 1956 the song ''Heartbreak Hotel'' rocked the music world, and practically overnight Elvis Presley, RCA's newest recording star, became a household name.

Elvis became so popular that later in 1956, Elvis' business manager, the crafty and shrewd Colonel Tom Parker, had Elvis copyrighted and incorporated into that which became known as Elvis Presley Enterprises.

Soon after the formation of Elvis Presley Enterprises, Colonel Parker recruited the services of a very successful businessman and promoter by the name of Hank Saperstein. What followed was one of the most successful mass marketing ventures ever devised.

With the business direction of Colonel Parker and the marketing genius of Hank Saperstein, Elvis Presley Enterprises issued a limited number of licenses to manufacturers for the production of an array of merchandise bearing Elvis' name and likeness. Everything from clothing and footwear, to school supplies and jewelry was available to the public — not to mention board games, dolls, and bubble gum cards.

In fact, by the time Elvis Presley Enterprises halted production of these items in 1957, there were well over sixty different pieces of merchandise available for the Elvis fan to choose from. To no surprise, sales from Elvis merchandising were so impressive that it prompted several manufacturers from England to request and receive permission from Elvis Presley Enterprises to manufacture Elvis items in their own country.

In conclusion, this mass marketing scheme not only proved to be a staggering financial success, but it also provided the spark that ignited the career of a young Elvis Presley, who would eventually become the greatest star the world of entertainment has ever known.

INTRODUCTION

In 1982, the first edition of **Elvis Collectibles** was introduced to the many legions of fans and collectors of Elvis memorabilia. Then in 1987, a new revised edition of **Elvis Collectibles** was published with newly discovered material, as well as an updated price guide.

In the past, the authors of **Elvis Collectibles** have attempted to offer the most comprehensive work on Elvis memorabilia available. The authors of **Elvis Collectibles** hope the reader has enjoyed these past two works and has found them beneficial in their search of Elvis memorabilia.

Now, fifteen years after the death of the late great Elvis Presley, the authors of **Elvis Collectibles** wish to commemorate this very special occasion by offering **The Best of Elvis Collectibles.**

The Best of Elvis Collectibles is designed to give the Elvis fan and collector an opportunity to view up close, in wonderful detail, many of the rarest and most sought after collectibles in existence regarding Elvis memorabilia.

So sit back and enjoy your journey through **The Best of Elvis Collectibles.**

CONTENTS

Elvis Presley Enterprises 1

RCA & Sun 33

Sheet Music & Photographs 43

Las Vegas & Concerts 51

Movies 59

Publications 79

Novelties 97

Advertisements 101

ELVIS PRESLEY

ENTERPRISES

Illustration 1 — 1956 ELVIS PRESLEY ENTERPRISES BOOKENDS
This single bookend stands approximately 7″ high and was finished in glossy ivory.
Manufactured by Sanjan Co.

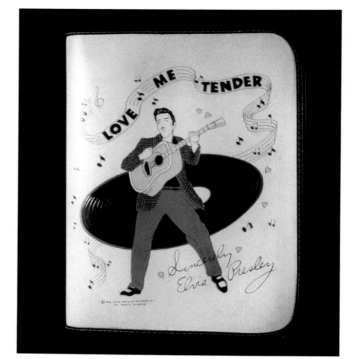

Illustration 2 —
1956 ELVIS PRESLEY ENTERPRISES
ZIPPER SCHOOL BINDER

Illustration 3 — 1956 ELVIS PRESLEY PENCILS
This pack of twelve pencils originally sold for 39 cents.
Also illustrated are the shipping box that contained the pencils and the pre-price tag.

Illustration 4 — 1956 ELVIS PRESLEY ENTERPRISES ZIPPER SCHOOL BINDER
Another color variation of the zipper school binder.
*Note: A three-ring binder was also available.

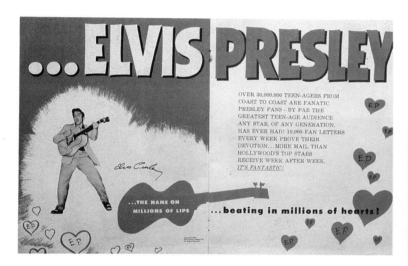

Illustration 5 — 1956 ELVIS PRESLEY ENTERPRISES "MR. TEENAGER"
This 16-page promotion booklet was sent to soft drink manufacturers. The promotion concept was to let Elvis advertise the product. For some reason this promotion was scratched.

**Illustration 6A — 1956 ELVIS PRESLEY ENTERPRISES
PICTURES WITH MOLDED FRAMES**
Pictures measure 5″×7″. Each frame is marked on the back
with the 1956 Elvis Presley Enterprises copyright.

**Illustration 6B — 1956 ELVIS PRESLEY ENTERPRISES
PHOTO ALBUM, AUTOGRAPH BOOK, SCRAP BOOK, RECORD CASE AND DIARY**
Published by the S.K. Smith Company, Chicago, Illinois.
These items are often referred to as ''the pink items.''

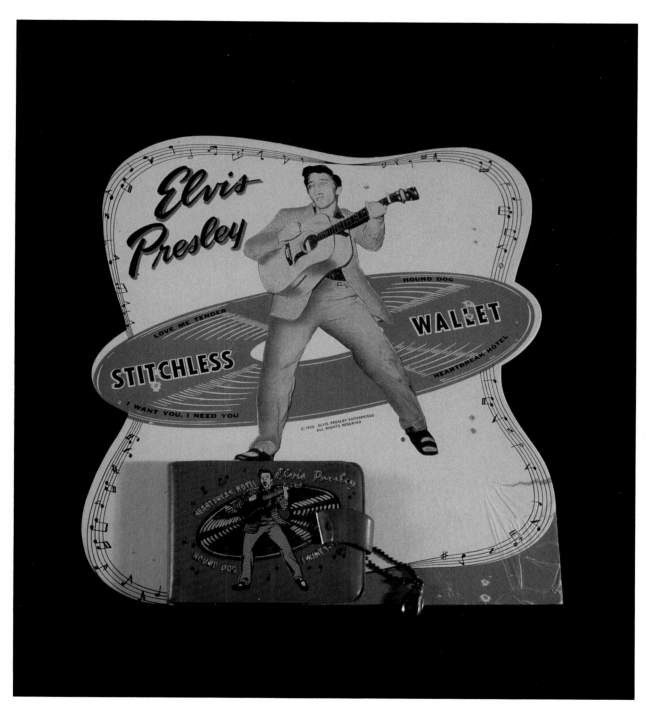

Illustration 7 — 1956 ELVIS PRESLEY ENTERPRISES WALLET DISPLAY CARD

Illustration 8 — 1956 ELVIS PRESLEY ENTERPRISES PLASTIC BELTS
These belts were available in various colors to match the wallets, billfolds, and French purse.

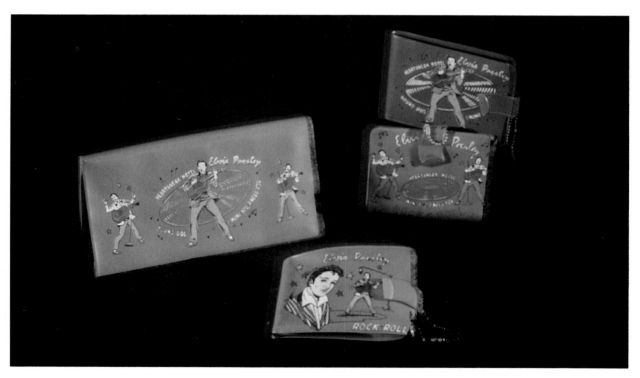

Illustration 9 — 1956 ELVIS PRESLEY ENTERPRISES
BILLFOLD, ROCK AND ROLL BILLFOLD, PHOTO WALLET, AND FRENCH PURSE
All of the above items were offered in various colors.

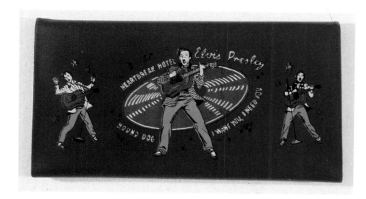

Illustration 10 — 1956 ELVIS PRESLEY ENTERPRISES FRENCH PURSE

Illustration 11 — 1956 ELVIS PRESLEY ENTERPRISES BILLFOLD

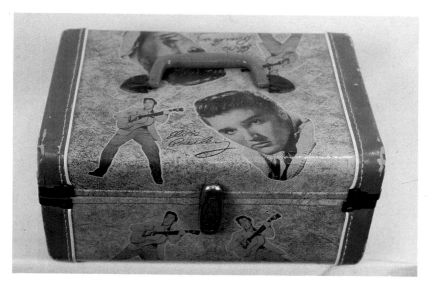

Illustration 12 — 1956 ELVIS PRESLEY ENTERPRISES OVERNIGHT CASE
Also available in brown.

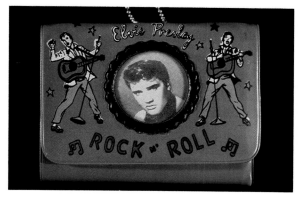

Illustration 13 — 1956 ELVIS PRESLEY ENTERPRISES PHOTO WALLET

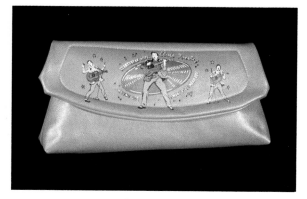

Illustration 14 — ELVIS PRESLEY ENTERPRISES CARRY ALL BAG

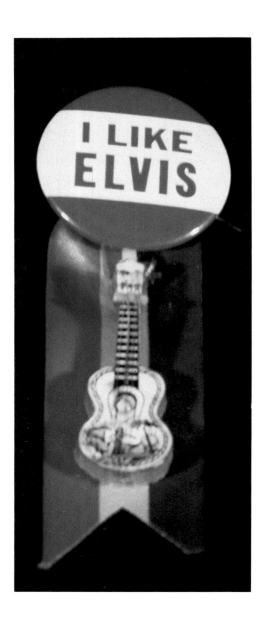

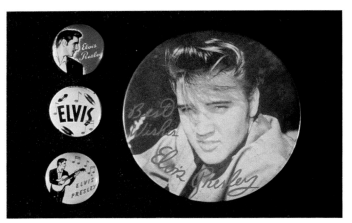

**Illustration 16 — 1956 ELVIS PRESLEY
ENTERPRISES PINBACK BUTTONS
AND CELLULOID PIN**
Marked 1956 E.P.E. — Green Duck Co., Chicago.

**Illustration 17 — LABEL FROM MACHINE
ADVERTISING ELVIS SIDEBURNS**

Illustration 15 — GUITAR PIN
Manufacturer unknown. Two other scenes
on guitar were also available.

**Illustration 18 — ELVIS PRESLEY ENTERPRISES
PINBACK BUTTONS**
Marked 1956 E.P.E. — Green Duck Co., Chicago.

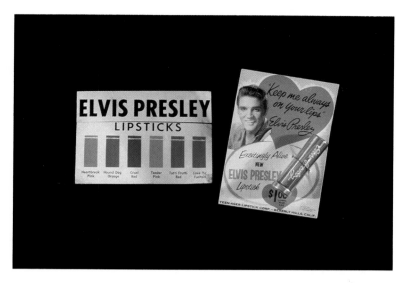

**Illustration 19 — 1956 ELVIS PRESLEY ENTERPRISES
LIPSTICK WITH LIPSTICK CHART**
Lipstick attached to original card is much in demand by collectors. The lipstick chart is very rare.
*Note: There is one other signature variation on the lipstick tube available.

**Illustration 20 — 1956 ELVIS PRESLEY ENTERPRISES
"TEDDY BEAR" PERFUME WITH THE ORIGINAL BOX**
*Note: A later and much different bottle style of "Teddy Bear" perfume was issued. Although it has a 1957 copyright date, the actual date it was issued is unknown.

Illustration 21 — 1956 ELVIS PRESLEY ENTERPRISES SCARF
The scarf measures 32″ square. Also available in a smaller kerchief and turban-style scarf.

Illustration 22 — 1956 ELVIS PRESLEY ENTERPRISES DOG TAG NECKLACE
The dog tag necklace in the complete package as illustrated is very rare.

**Illustration 23 — 1956 ELVIS PRESLEY ENTERPRISES
SWEATER HOLDER, "LOVE ME TENDER" NECKLACE, AND KEY CHAIN**
The necklace was also available in gold.

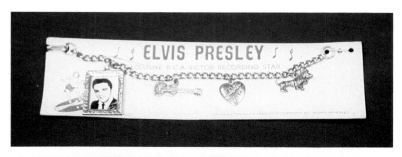

Illustration 24 — 1956 ELVIS PRESLEY CHARM BRACELETS
Although the bracelets are identical, the cards on which they are displayed not only differ in color, but also where they were printed. The blue card was "Printed in Canada," while the red card was "Printed in USA."
*Note: The charm bracelet was reproduced in 1977. The bracelets are similar except for framed photo.

**Illustration 25 — 1956 ELVIS PRESLEY EARRINGS, GUITAR PIN,
AND CHARM BRACELET**
The jewelry illustrated above may be the rarest jewelry items.

Illustration 26 — 1956 ELVIS PRESLEY ALUMINUM MEDALLION
A similar necklace of lighter weight was sold during Elvis' Las Vegas engagement in the '70s.

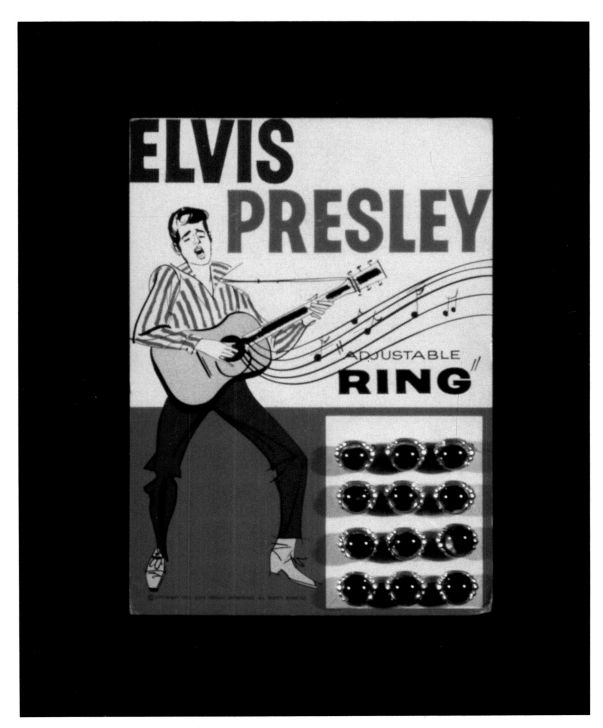

**Illustration 27 — ELVIS PRESLEY ENTERPRISES
ADJUSTABLE RINGS ON ORIGINAL DISPLAY CARD**
The Elvis Presley adjustable ring has a clear crystal cabochon covering a color photograph of
Elvis. The back of the ring reads ''ELVIS PRESLEY ENTERPRISES — all rights reserved.''

Illustration 28 — 1956 ELVIS PRESLEY ENTERPRISES ASHTRAY (OR) COASTER
Ashtray measures 3½ inches in diameter.

**Illustration 29 — 1956 ELVIS PRESLEY ENTERPRISES DRINKING GLASS
AND GLASS PLATE**
*Note: The 1956 drinking glass was reproduced in the '80s and bears an '80s copyright.

**Illustration 30 — 1956 ELVIS PRESLEY ENTERPRISES
"LOVE ME TENDER" PILLOW**
Pillow measures 10″ by 10″.

Illustration 31 — 1956 ELVIS PRESLEY ENTERPRISES THROW PILLOW
Pillow measures 10½″ by 10½″. It was also available in green and beige.

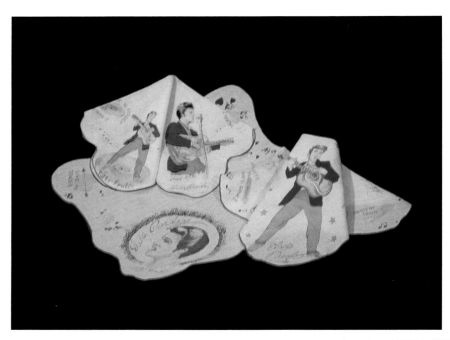

Illustration 32 — 1956 ELVIS PRESLEY ENTERPRISES HANDKERCHIEFS
These delicate and colorful handkerchiefs were available in three different prints. There were different color variations available.

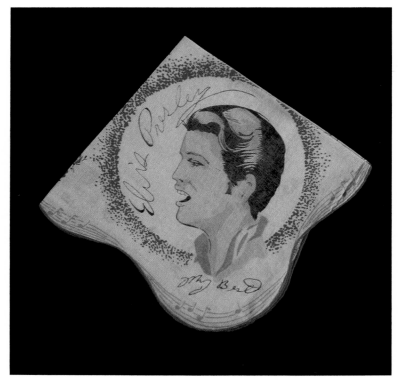

Illustration 33 — 1956 ELVIS PRESLEY ENTERPRISES HANDKERCHIEF
Another color variation of the handkerchief.

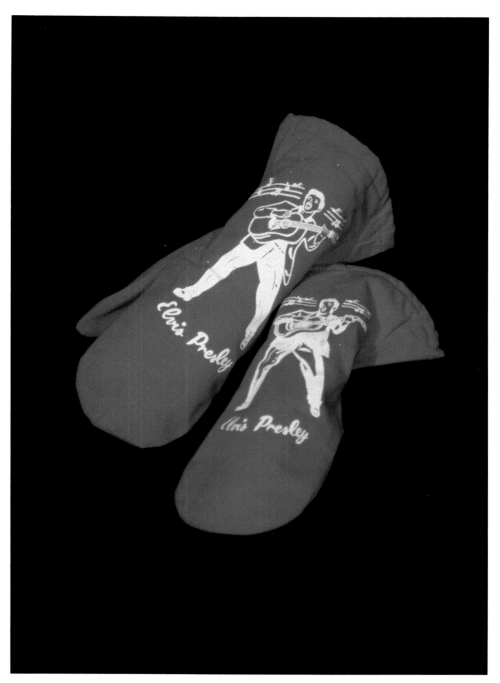

Illustration 34 — 1956 ELVIS PRESLEY ENTERPRISES MITTENS
Manufactured by Nolan Gloves. The mittens were available in red, white, and navy.

**Illustration 35 — 1956 ELVIS PRESLEY
ENTERPRISES TEE SHIRT**

**Illustration 36 — 1956 ELVIS PRESLEY
ENTERPRISES LEATHER BELT AND
ELVIS BELT BUCKLE**

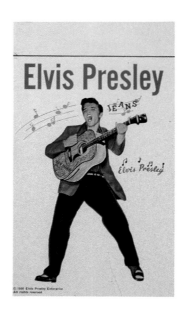

**Illustration 37 — 1956 ELVIS PRESLEY
ENTERPRISES BLUE JEANS TAG**
This tag was folded and placed in back pocket of the Elvis Presley jeans. The tag was the only identification to show they were authentic Elvis Presley jeans.

Illustration 38 — 1956 ELVIS PRESLEY ENTERPRISES CREW HAT WITH PINS
The hat was manufactured by Magnet Company, N.Y., N.Y. Pinback buttons measure $\frac{7}{8}''$
and are marked 1956 E.P.E. — Green Duck Co., Chicago.

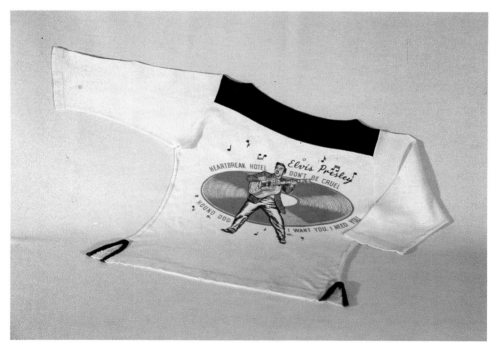

Illustration 39 — 1956 ELVIS PRESLEY ENTERPRISES BOAT NECK SHIRT
The boat neck was also available in green.

Illustration 40 — 1956 ELVIS PRESLEY ENTERPRISES FELT SKIRT
Manufactured by Little Jean Togs, Inc. The skirt was also available in denim and corduroy.

Illustration 41 — 1956 ELVIS PRESLEY ENTERPRISES PUMP SHOES
WITH ORIGINAL BOX
Manufactured by Faith Shoe Co. Available in leather and fabric.

**Illustration 42 — 1956 ELVIS PRESLEY ENTERPRISES SNEAKERS
AND SNEAKER BOX**
Manufactured by Randolph Manufacturing Company. The sneakers are rare and highly sought after by collectors. The shoe box, however, is considered extremely rare.

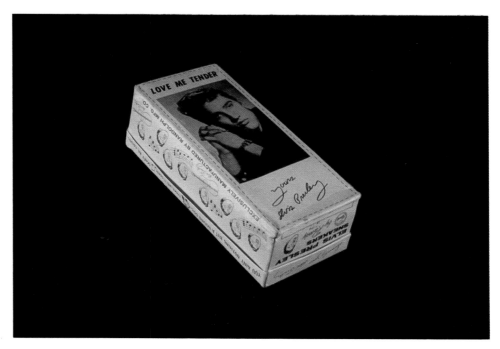

Illustration 42A — 1956 ELVIS PRESLEY ENTERPRISES SNEAKER BOX
This illustration displays the bottom of the sneaker box.

Illustration 43 — 1956 ELVIS PRESLEY ENTERPRISES STATUETTE
This 8″ bronzed plastic statue originally sold for $1.00. Considered very rare.

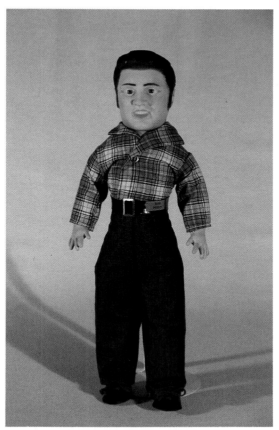

**Illustration 44 and 44A — 1957 ELVIS PRESLEY ENTERPRISES
DOLL IN ORIGINAL BOX**

Doll is eighteen inches tall and has a soft "magic skin" body. The original clothes include a plaid shirt, blue pants, black belt, and a pair of "blue suede shoes." The belt originally had an orange sticker with "Elvis Presley" written on it. Definitely one of the rarest and most sought after Elvis Collector items.

*Note: There is quite possibly a shirt variation for the doll.

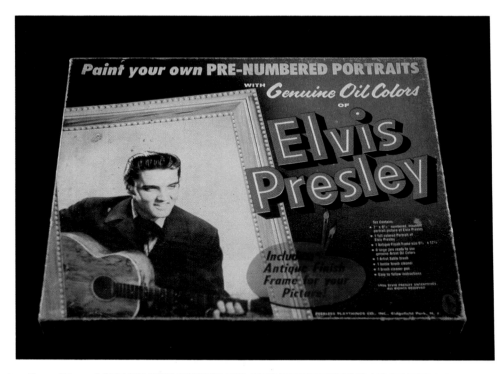

Illustration 45 — 1957 ELVIS PRESLEY ENTERPRISES PAINT BY NUMBER SET
Definitely one of the rarest and most sought after Elvis items.
Manufactured by Peerless Playthings Co., Richfield Park, New Jersey.

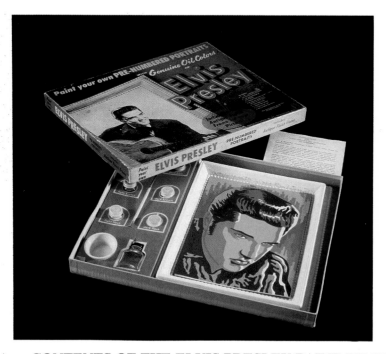

Illustration 45A — CONTENTS OF THE ELVIS PRESLEY PAINT BY NUMBER SET

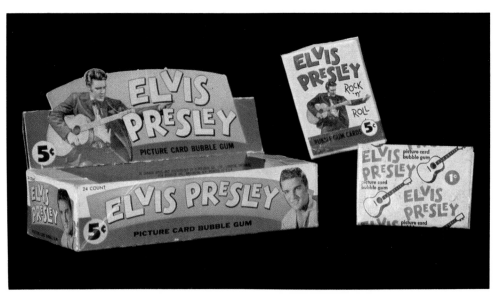

**Illustration 46 — 1956 ELVIS PRESLEY ENTERPRISES BUBBLE GUM BOX
AND GUM WRAPPERS**

Illustration 47 — 1956 ELVIS PRESLEY ENTERPRISES BUBBLE GUM CARDS
Complete set consisted of 66 cards. The last twenty cards featured color scenes from Elvis'
first movie, ''Love Me Tender.''

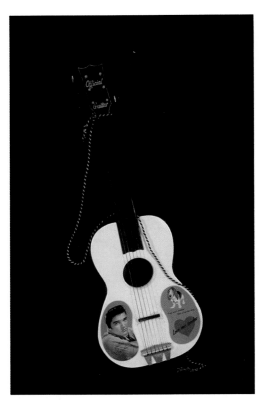

Illustration 48 — 1956 ELVIS PRESLEY ENTERPRISES SIX-STRING GUITAR

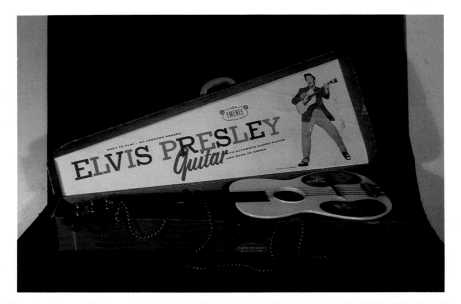

**Illustration 48A — 1956 ELVIS PRESLEY ENTERPRISES GUITAR
WITH CARRYING CASE**

Two different E.P.E. guitars were manufactured by Emenee. The four-string guitar came with carrying case, song book, and chord player. However, the six-string guitar apparently came with only the carrying case.

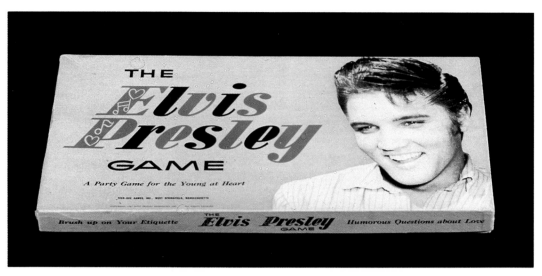

Illustration 49 — 1956 ELVIS PRESLEY ENTERPRISES BOARD GAME
This highly sought after item originally sold for $3.49. The theme of the game was ''love.''

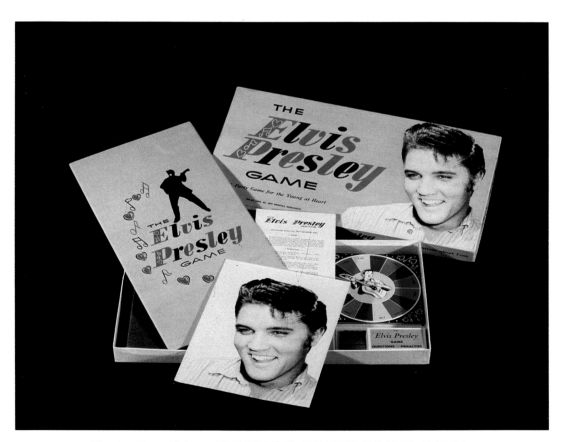

Illustration 49A — CONTENTS OF THE BOARD GAME
The game contained a playing board, spinner, playing pieces, and a free 8″ × 10″ black and white photo of Elvis.

Illustration 50 — 1961 ELVIS PRESLEY ENTERPRISES GOLD BUST
This extremely rare pewter bust stands 7″ high and has a 2½″ by 2″ base. The gold bust may be the only 1961 EPE item available.

Illustration 51 — 1957 ELVIS PRESLEY ENTERPRISES PROMOTIONAL PHOTO
This photo was also available with a blue border and was offered in two different sizes, 8″ × 10″ and 11″ × 14″.

Illustration 52 — 1957 ELVIS PRESLEY ENTERPRISES
"JOHN'S POCKET MOVIE"

By flipping the pages of this booklet, a "life action" simulation of Elvis dancing from a movie scene in "Jailhouse Rock" was created.

*Note: Controversy surrounds this item in regard to origin and the late discovery of this item by many collectors.

Illustration 53 — 1956 ELVIS PRESLEY ENTERPRISES PHOTO
IN MOLDED FRAME, HOT PLATE, AND CELLULOID PINS
Two other photos in molded frames were also available.

This 1956 Elvis Presley Enterprises glow-in-the-dark photograph is worth $225.00.

R C A & S U N

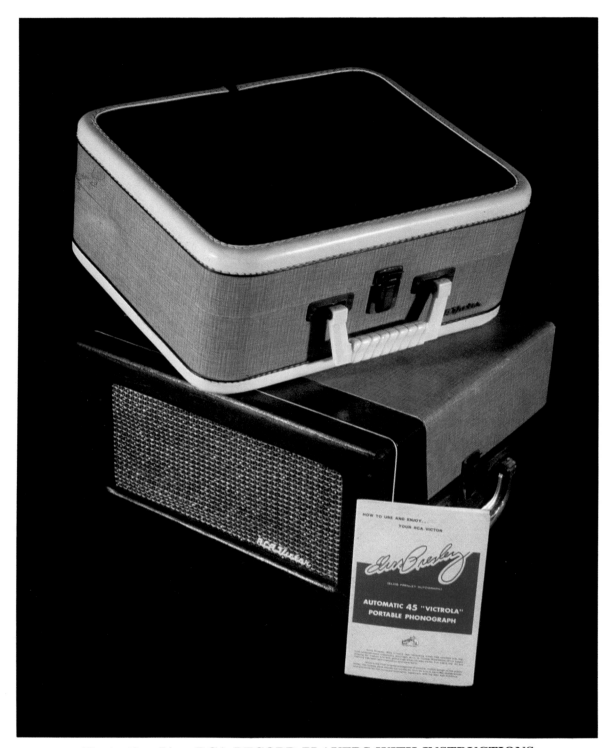

Illustration 54 — RCA RECORD PLAYERS WITH INSTRUCTIONS
These two models of "Elvis Presley Autograph" record players were issued in 1956 and marketed by RCA. The only distinguishing mark is a gold inlay of Elvis' autograph on the top cover. The top model is the 4-speed model, while the automatic 45 is shown on the bottom.

Illustration 55 — RCA BONUS PHOTOS
RCA bonus photos were an added feature included with the purchase of many of Elvis' long play record albums. Beginning center then moving left to right: 1963 calendar from ''Girls, Girls, Girls,'' ''It Happened at the World's Fair,'' ''Elvis Sings Burning Love,'' and ''Elvis' Golden Records, Volume 4.''

ELVIS PRESLEY

Exclusive RCA Victor
Recording Artist

Illustration 56 — "KING CREOLE" BONUS PHOTO
This 8″ × 10″ black and white photo was a bonus giveway for a limited time with the purchase
of the "King Creole" album.

Illustration 57 — RCA 1963 POCKET CALENDAR
This is the first and rarest of all the pocket calendars that were issued by RCA from 1963 through 1980.
*Note: In 1980 RCA issued authentic reproductions of the originals. However, the color on the back is a variation from the original.

Illustration 57A —
COMPLETE SET OF ORIGINAL RCA POCKET CALENDARS

Illustration 58 — ELVIS CHRISTMAS CARDS
Beginning from bottom left moving outside and coming down: (a) 1975; (b) 1958; (c) 1967; (d) 1974; (e) 1960; (f) 1959; (g) 1961; (h) 1966; (i) 1971; (j) middle left — 1963; (k) middle up — 1968; (l) middle right — 1972.

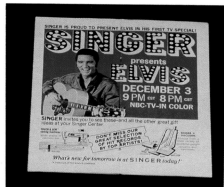

Illustration 59 — 1968 SINGER TV SPECIAL CATALOG

Catalog lists the television stations that carried the Singer TV special on December 3, 1968. The catalog measures 4″ × 9″ and contains 32 pages. The illustrations above show the front cover, middle, and back cover.

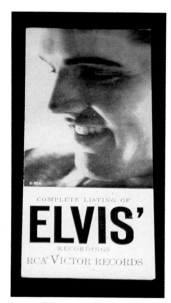

Illustration 61

ELVIS 1959 RECORD CATALOG

Illustration 60 — 1956 CONCERT TICKET

This ticket was to be used for the Elvis Presley concert on Sunday March 18, 1956, at the County Hall Auditorium in Charleston, S.C.

Illustration 62 — ALOHA TICKET

This unused ticket is from the now **historic** Aloha concert in which Elvis performed via satellite on January 14, 1973, from Honolulu, Hawaii.

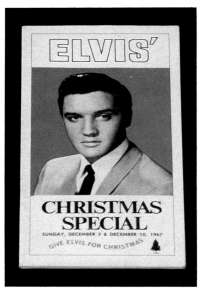

Illustration 63 & 64 — RCA CHRISTMAS POSTER AND CATALOG
This poster served two purposes. It promoted Elvis' Christmas records and also promoted the Elvis Christmas Special that was broadcast on radio for Christmas, 1967. The catalog gave information regarding the '67 Christmas Special.

ELVIS PRESLEY

Illustration 65 — ELVIS PUBLICITY PHOTO
This is possibly the first SUN promotional photograph of Elvis.

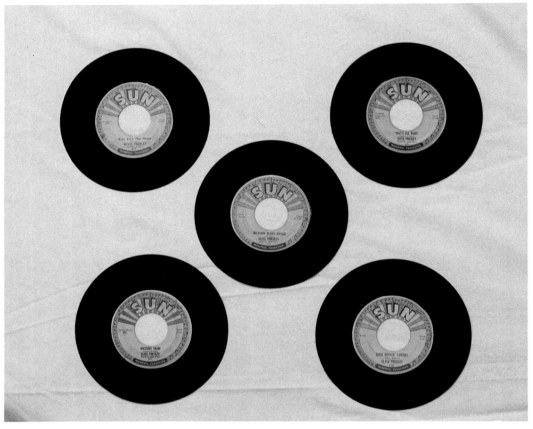

Illustration 66 — ELVIS ON SUN

From a historical point of view the five SUNs illustrated above certainly rank among everyone's best. Depending on the condition of these precious vinyls, they are no doubt a wonderful investment.

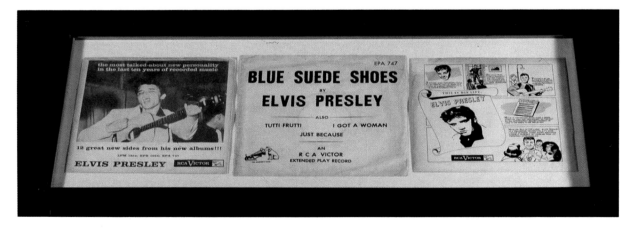

Illustration 67 — ELVIS PICTURE SLEEVES

These extremely rare picture sleeves are not only highly collectible for record collectors, but for memorabilia collectors as well. Beginning from left to right: RCA EPB-1254; RCA EPA-747; "This is His Life" picture sleeve.

SHEET MUSIC & PHOTOGRAPHS

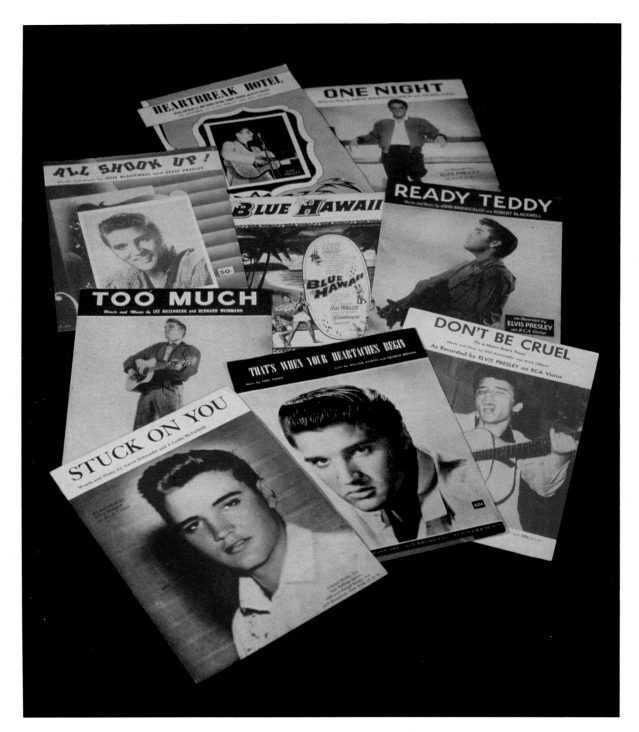

Illustration 68 — SHEET MUSIC COLLAGE

An illustration of many of the rarer and harder to find pieces of Elvis' sheet music. Beginning from bottom left going up and coming down: "Stuck on You", "Too Much", "All Shook Up", "Heartbreak Hotel", "One Night", "Ready Teddy", "Don't Be Cruel", and "That's When Your Heartaches Begin"; center: "Blue Hawaii".

Illustration 69 — "OLD SHEP" SHEET MUSIC

Illustration 70 — ELVIS SHEET MUSIC —
"I DON'T CARE IF THE SUN DON'T SHINE"

"I Don't Care if the Sun Don't Shine" is believed to be the only piece of sheet music that represents a song originally recorded by Elvis on SUN RECORDS which bears his photograph. It was issued when RCA released the song on its own label in 1956.

Illustration 71 — ELVIS SHEET MUSIC — "ELVIS PRESLEY FOR PRESIDENT"
Also extremely rare and sought after because of its cartoon-like design, and of course, for the fact it does not relate to anything recorded by Elvis, but by singer Lou Monte. There is also a blue and white tab pin that promoted the record, "Elvis Presley for President" by Lou Monte which reads, "ELVIS PRESLEY FOR PRESIDENT, LOU MONTE CAMPAIGN MANAGER."

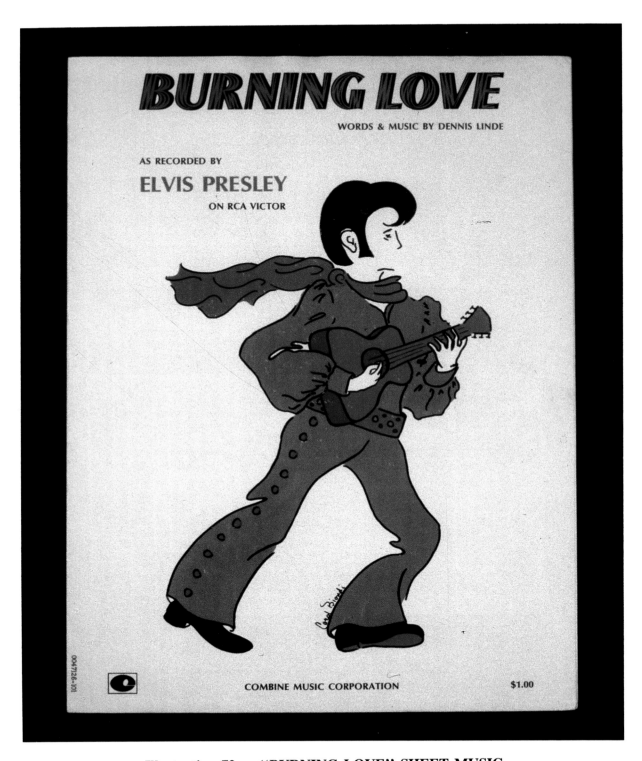

Illustration 72 — "BURNING LOVE" SHEET MUSIC
This is the only piece of Elvis sheet music that featured a cartoon likeness of Elvis rather than a photograph.

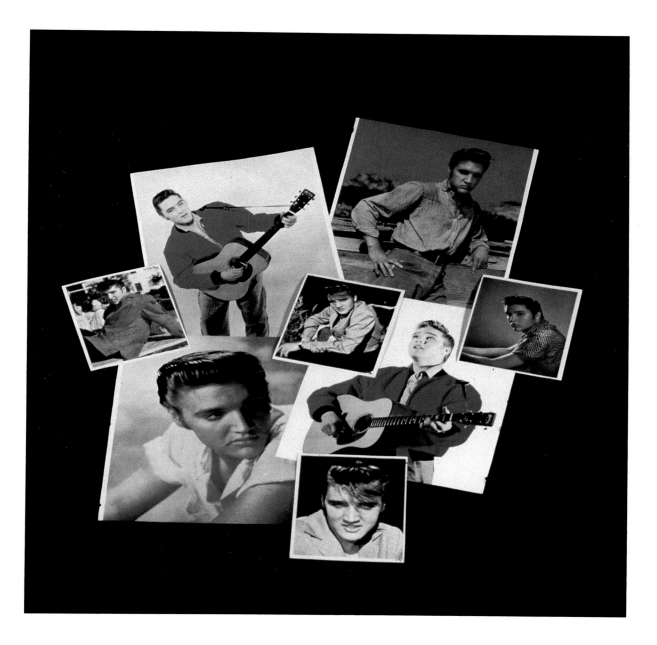

Illustration 73 — COLLAGE OF TWO PHOTO SETS
The smaller pictures measure 4″ × 5″ and were sold through the mail in 1956. The larger pictures measure 8″ × 10″ and were also available by mail order in 1956.

Illustration 74 — ELVIS PASTEL PHOTOGRAPHS
These 8″ × 10″ pastel color tinted photographs sold in 1956.

LAS VEGAS & CONCERTS

Illustration 75 — LAS VEGAS AND CONCERT COLLAGE

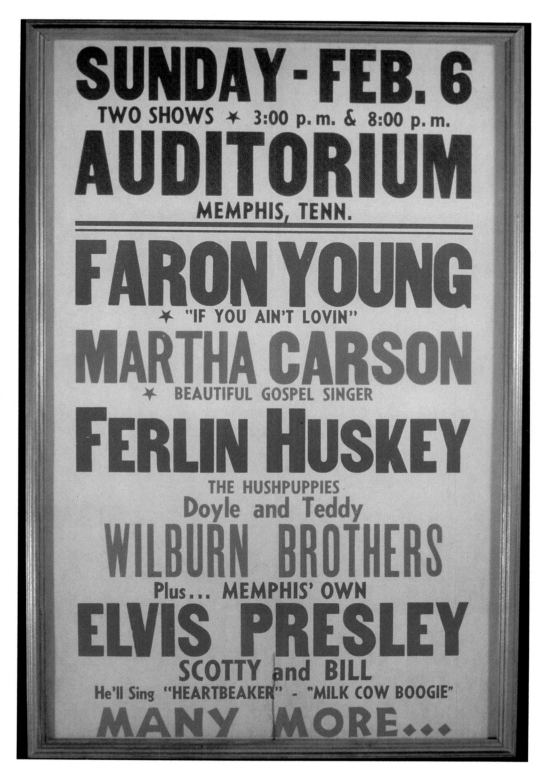

Illustration 76 — ELVIS 1955 CONCERT POSTER
This poster measures 14″ × 22″.

Illustration 77 — TOUR PHOTO ALBUMS
Beginning lower left moving clockwise: Elvis Presley ''Mr. Dynamite'', Elvis Presley ''Mr. Rhythm'', and Elvis Presley ''Photo Folio''.

The photo programs listed on this page are in great demand by collectors. Although there are earlier programs featuring Elvis, these are the first tour programs in which Elvis dominated the cover, as well as the contents.

''Mr. Rhythm'' is considered the first tour program. However, ''Mr. Dynamite'' is the first ''all Elvis'' program. ''Elvis Presley'' photo album featured in the lower right illustration is third and Elvis Presley ''Photo Folio'' is fourth. The ''Photo Folio'' is marked with the 1957 EPE copyright and was available with two different back covers.

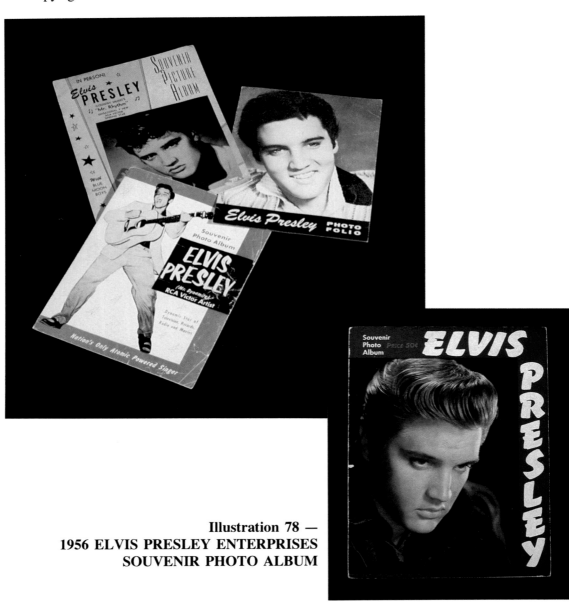

**Illustration 78 —
1956 ELVIS PRESLEY ENTERPRISES
SOUVENIR PHOTO ALBUM**

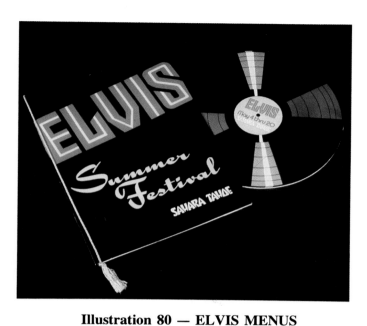

Illustration 80 — ELVIS MENUS
The menu illustrated on the left was used for the July 20-August 2, 1971, Sahara Tahoe Hotel engagement. It measures 9″ × 12″. The menu on the right was used for the May 4-May 20, 1973, engagement at the Sahara Tahoe Hotel. This menu measures 9¾″ in diameter.

Illustration 79 — ELVIS MENU
This menu was used for the first Elvis Las Vegas engagement in 1969. The engagement was at the International Hotel which is now the Las Vegas Hilton.

Illustration 81 — ELVIS MENU
Elvis menu from the Las Vegas Hilton engagement December 2-15, 1975. Menu measures 7″ × 16⅞″.

Illustration 82 — ELVIS PENNANTS
Various Elvis pennants that sold at Elvis' concerts in the 1970s.

Illustration 83 — ELVIS SOUVENIRS
Souvenirs from Vegas and Tahoe engagements.

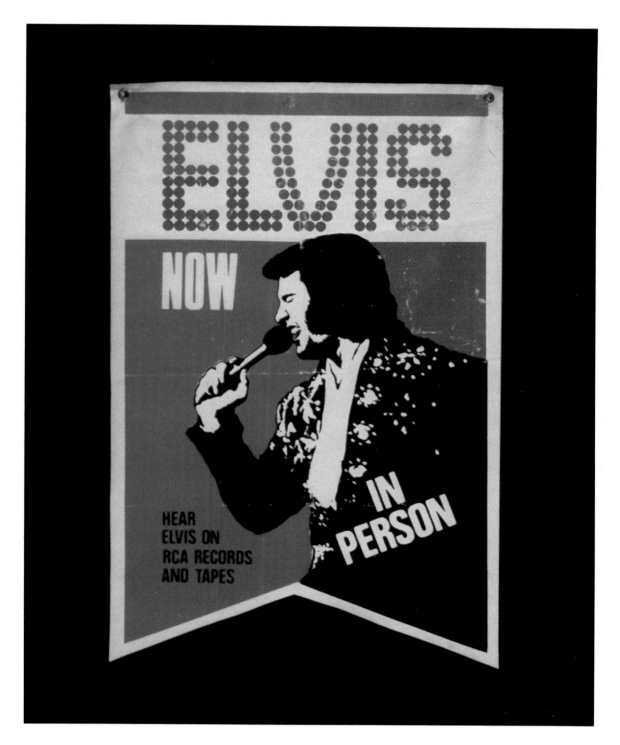

Illustration 84 — ELVIS OIL CLOTH BANNER
This oil cloth banner was hung in the lobby of the Hilton Hotel during Elvis' Las Vegas engagements.

Illustration 85 — INTERNATIONAL HOTEL POSTER
This cardboard poster hung in the lobby of the International Hotel promoting Elvis' engagement there in August of 1969.

MOVIES

Illustration 86 — ELVIS' MOVIE COLLAGE

Illustration 87 — "LOVE ME TENDER" MOVIE BANNER

Illustration 88 — "LOVING YOU" MOVIE BANNER

Illustration 89 — "JAILHOUSE ROCK" MOVIE BANNER

Illustration 90 —

"LOVE ME TENDER" PRESS BOOK

Illustration 91 —

"LOVING YOU" PRESS BOOK

Illustration 92 —

"JAILHOUSE ROCK" PRESS BOOK

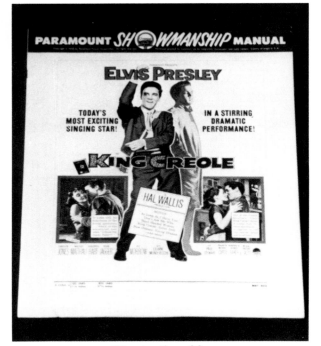

Illustration 93 —

"KING CREOLE" PRESS BOOK

*Note: There was also an Advance Press Book for "Jailhouse Rock" and a Reissue Press Book for "King Creole".

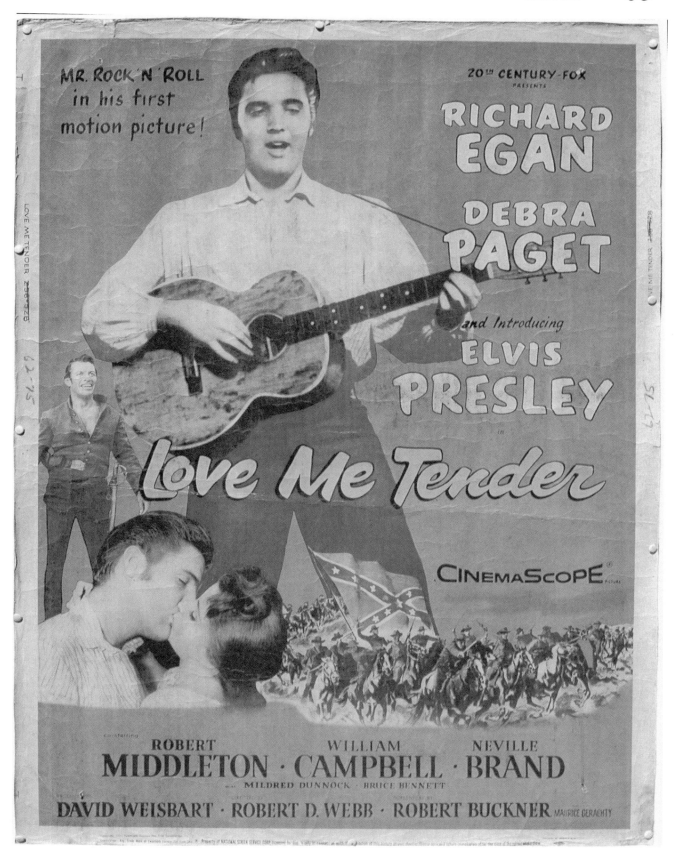

Illustration 94 — 30″ × 40″ POSTER FROM "LOVE ME TENDER"

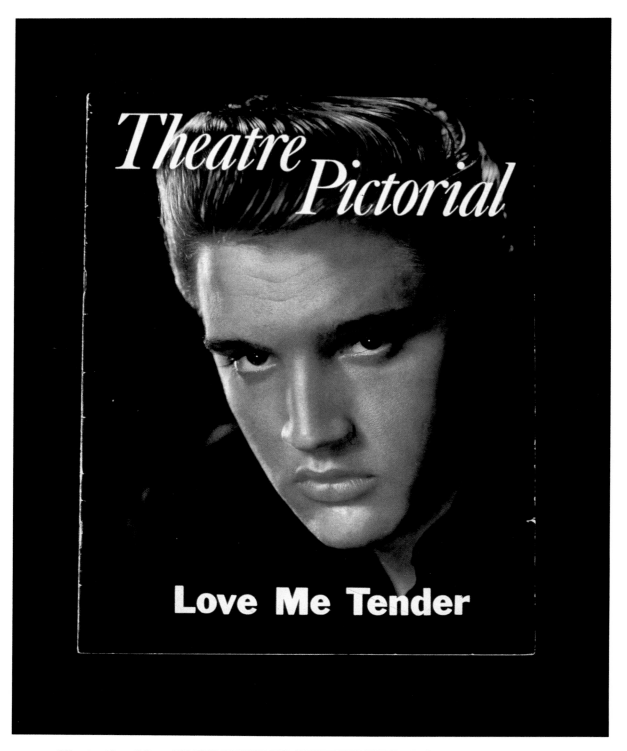

**Illustration 95 — ELVIS PRESLEY ENTERPRISES "LOVE ME TENDER"
THEATRE PICTORIAL**
The "Love Me Tender" theatre pictorial sold originally for fifty cents. The pictorial sold at
both movie houses and through magazine advertisements.

Illustration 96 — LOBBY CARDS FROM THE MOVIE "LOVE ME TENDER"

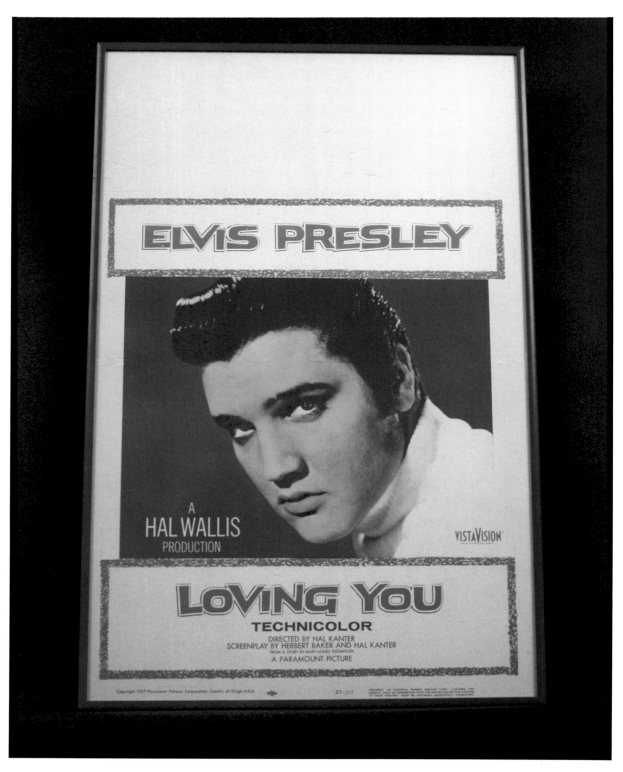

Illustration 97 — "LOVING YOU" WINDOW CARD
One of the most unusual movie pieces available.

Illustration 98 — "LOVING YOU" LOBBY PHOTO
This 22″ × 28″ poster is referred to as the B-style since there was one other lobby photo for this movie.

Illustration 99 — "LOVING YOU" ONE SHEET
Poster measures 27″ × 41″.

Illustration 100 — 11″ × 14″ LOBBY CARDS FROM "LOVING YOU"

**Illustration 101 — LOBBY CARDS
FROM THE MOVIE "LOVING YOU"
(REISSUE) 1959**

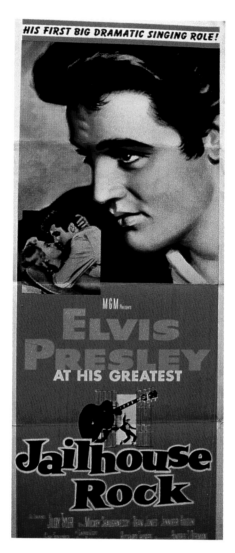

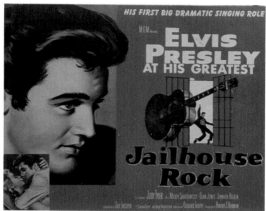

Illustration 103 —
"JAILHOUSE ROCK"
LOBBY CARDS

Illustration 102 —
"JAILHOUSE ROCK"
INSERT POSTER

Illustration 104 —
"JAILHOUSE ROCK"
WINDOW CARD POSTER

Illustration 105 — "KING CREOLE" LOBBY PHOTO POSTER
This is the original 22″ × 28″ poster ad for "King Creole".

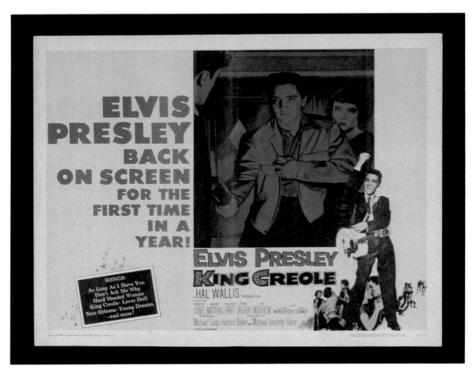

Illustration 106 — "KING CREOLE REISSUE" LOBBY PHOTO POSTER
This is the reissue 22″ × 28″ poster ad for "King Creole".

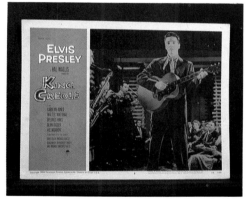

**Illustration 107 —
ORIGINAL LOBBY CARD
FROM THE MOVIE "KING CREOLE"**

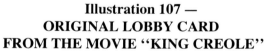

**Illustration 108 — COMPLETE SET OF REISSUE LOBBY CARDS
FROM "KING CREOLE"**

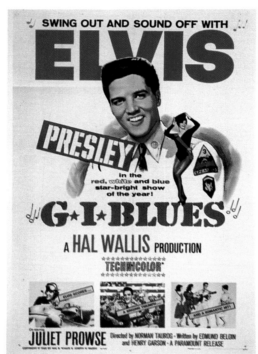

Illustration 109 —
"G.I. BLUES" ONE SHEET POSTER

Illustration 110 — "G.I. BLUES" LOBBY CARDS

Illustration 111 —
"BLUE HAWAII" ONE SHEET POSTER

Illustration 112 — "BLUE HAWAII" LOBBY CARDS

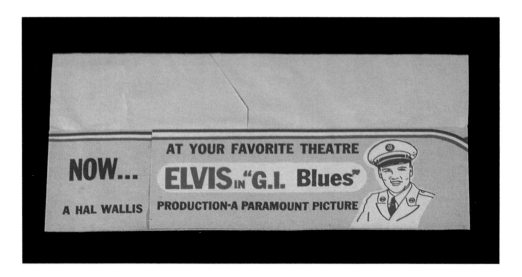

Illustration 113 — "G.I. BLUES" HAT

Issued in 1960. The opposite side of the hat reads "Available at RCA Victor Dealers/Elvis' G.I. Blues Album." The hat was issued with a blue card that measures 2⅜″ by 4⅛″ and reads "Keep This".

Illustration 114 — "BLUE HAWAII" LEI MEDALLION

The Hawaiian medallion served a dual purpose by promoting the movie and RCA soundtrack of the same title "Blue Hawaii". Medallion measures 5″ in diameter.

*Note: There is also a medallion which reads "see Blue Hawaii/A Hal Wallis Production starring Elvis Presley".

Illustration 115 — "JAILHOUSE ROCK" HERALD

**Illustration 116 —
"LOVE ME TENDER" STANDEE**

**Illustration 117 —
"LOVING YOU" STANDEE**

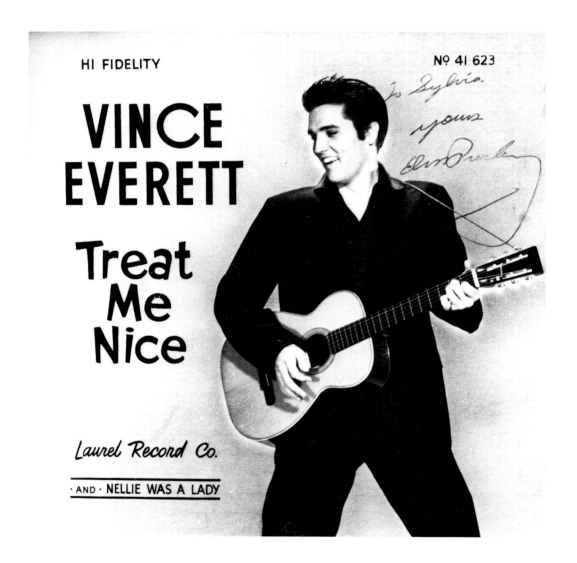

Illustration 118 — "JAILHOUSE ROCK" MOVIE PROP
This record sleeve was used as a movie prop in the record shop scene in "Jailhouse Rock".

PUBLICATIONS

Illustration 119 — ELVIS ROCK AND ROLL MAGAZINES

Beginning from bottom left going up and coming down: *Teenage Rock and Roll Review,* December 1956; *Teenage Rock and Roll Review,* October 1956; *COOL,* April 1957; *Rock 'N Roll Stars* #2, 1957; *Rock 'N Roll Stars* #1, 1956; *TEEN LIFE,* April 1957; *16 Magazine* ''The Elvis Diary'', May 1957.

Illustration 120 — ELVIS PRESLEY COMIC BOOK
Young Lovers was published by Charlton Publications in 1957. This comic featured a two page
''copy'' story titled, ''The Real Elvis Presley Complete Life Story''.

Illustration 121 — ELVIS IN THE ARMY
This illustration is to commemorate Elvis' army years. Pictured are just a few of the many magazines in which Elvis donned the cover in his military issue. Special attention is given to the magazine titled *Elvis in the Army* by Ideal Corp., 1959.

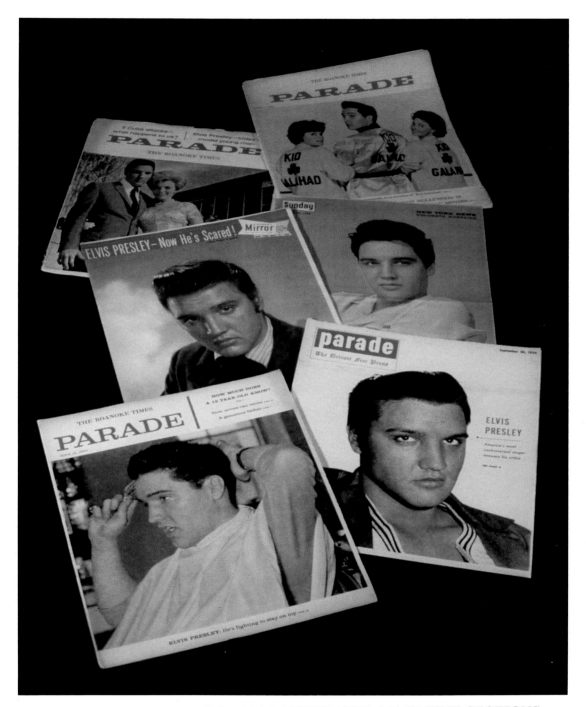

Illustration 122 — ELVIS SUNDAY NEWSPAPER MAGAZINE SECTIONS
These rare and hard to find items were bonus sections in Sunday newspapers found across America.

Beginning from bottom left going up and coming down: *Roanoke Times Parade,* June 19, 1960; *Sunday Mirror,* November 11, 1956; *Roanoke Times Parade,* November 4, 1962; *Roanoke Times Parade,* March 11, 1962; *New York News, Coloroto Magazine,* April 20, 1958; and *Parade* from *Detroit Free Press,* September 30, 1956.

Illustration 123 — ELVIS SUNDAY MIRROR
This beautiful and unusual picture graced the cover of the *Sunday Mirror* magazine section in New York on February 17, 1957.

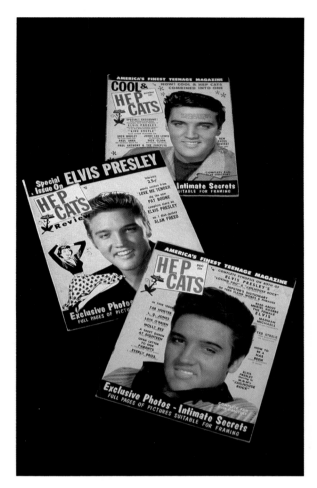

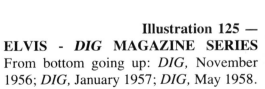

Illustration 124 —
ELVIS - *HEP CATS* MAGAZINE SERIES
From bottom going up: *Hep Cats*, December
1957; *Hep Cats Review*, February 1956; *Cool
& Hep Cats*, October 1958.

Illustration 125 —
ELVIS - *DIG* MAGAZINE SERIES
From bottom going up: *DIG*, November
1956; *DIG*, January 1957; *DIG*, May 1958.

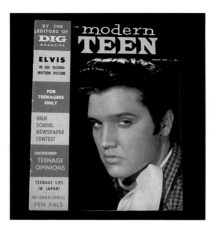

Illustration 128
MODERN TEEN

Illustration 127
ROCK AND ROLL ROUNDUP

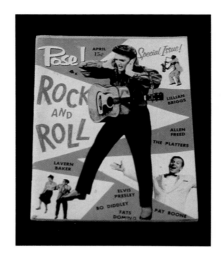

Illustration 130
POSE!

Illustration 129
TEEN

Illustration 126
TRUE STRANGE

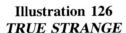

Illustrations 126-130 — ELVIS MAGAZINES
These hard to find magazines are treasured by collectors for their artistic covers. From bottom going clockwise: *True Strange*, June 1957; *Rock and Roll Roundup*, April 1957; *Modern Teen*, August 1957; *Teen*, June 1958; and center: *Pose!*, April 1957.

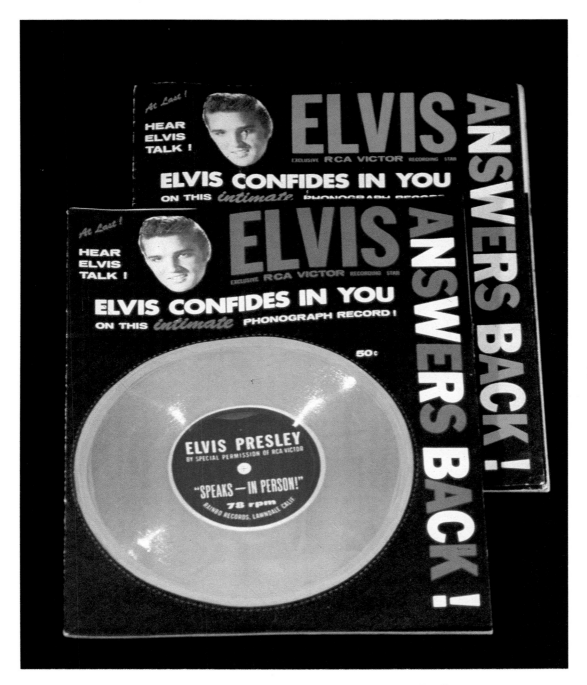

Illustration 131 — "ELVIS ANSWERS BACK"

Distributed by Sound Publishing Co., Laundale, California, 1956. This magazine was issued with two different record labels and two different color schemes for the cover. The magazine with the red and white letters is labeled *Elvis Presley — Speaks in Person*. The magazine with the green and white letters is labeled *Elvis Presley — The Truth About Me!*

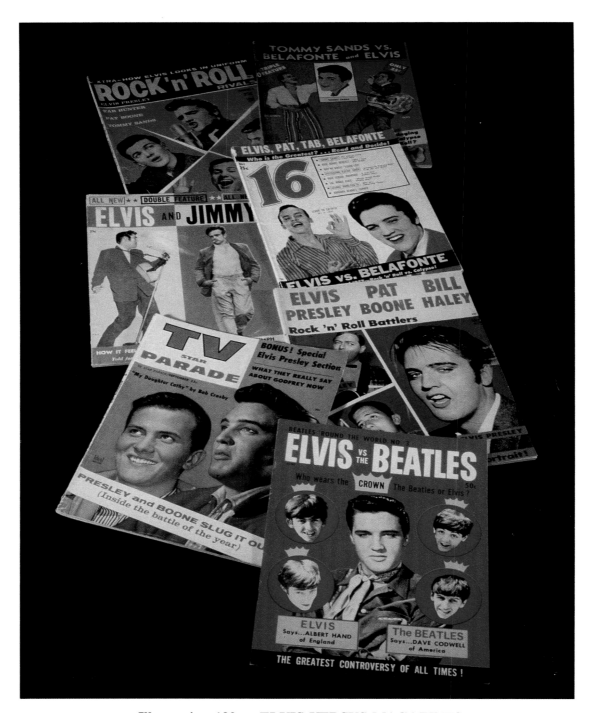

Illustration 132 — ELVIS VERSUS MAGAZINES
These popular Elvis Magazines had Elvis opposing other popular stars in the '50s and '60s. Beginning from bottom left going up and coming down: *TV Star Parade*, September 1956; *Elvis and Jimmy*, 1956; *Rock 'n Roll Rivals #1*, 1957; *Tommy Sands vs. Belafonte and Elvis*, 1957; *16 Magazine*, July 1957; *Rock 'n Roll Battler*, December 1956; *Elvis vs. the Beatles*, 1965.

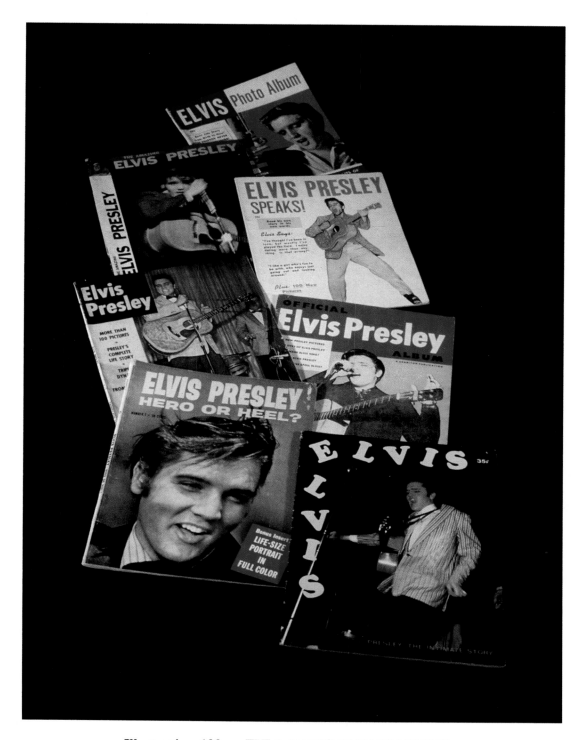

Illustration 133 — FULL ELVIS PUBLICATIONS
The magazines illustrated above pertain only to Elvis Presley. Beginning from bottom left going up and coming down: *Elvis Presley — Hero or Heel*, 1956; *Elvis Presley*, 1956; *The Amazing Elvis Presley*, 1956; *Elvis Photo Album*, 1956; *Elvis Presley Speaks*, 1956; *Official Elvis Presley Album*, 1956; *Elvis - The Intimate Story*, 1956.

Illustration 137
COUNTRY SONG ROUNDUP
February 1957

Illustration 136
THE CASH BOX
March 18, 1961

Illustration 138
COWBOY SONGS #48
1956

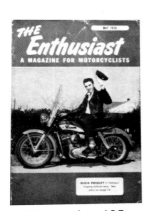

Illustration 135
THE ENTHUSIAST
May 1956

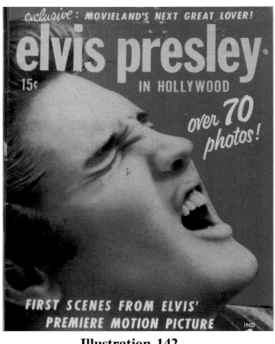

Illustration 142
ELVIS IN HOLLYWOOD
1956
Measures 4½″ × 5½″

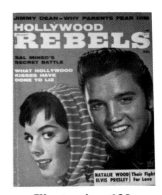

Illustration 139
HOLLYWOOD REBELS
1957

Illustration 134
TV RADIO MIRROR
December 1956

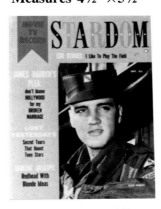

Illustration 141
STARDOM
September 1959

Illustration 140
FILMS AND FILMING
August 1966

Illustration 143 — NEW YORK SUNDAY NEWS COLOROTO MAGAZINE
Issued June 24, 1956.

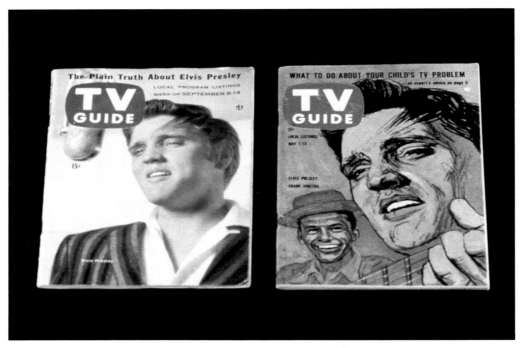

Illustration 144 — ELVIS ON *TV GUIDE* COVERS

Although there were other *TV Guide* magazines which featured stories on Elvis, the above illustration shows the only two in which Elvis' photograph or likeness dominated the cover during his career. The *TV Guide* on the left is the first time Elvis appeared on the cover of this magazine, issued September 8-14, 1956. The *TV Guide* on the right was issued May 7-13, 1960.

Illustration 145
CHICAGO TRIBUNE TV WEEK
Issued July 7-13, 1956

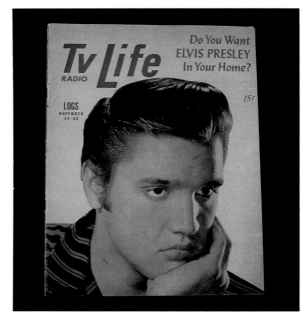

Illustration 146
RADIO TV LIFE
November 24-30, 1956

Illustration 147 — THE ELVIS PRESLEY STORY

Authored by James Gregory. Published in 1960 by Hillman Books. This was the first paperback on Elvis. A British version that was slightly different was published later.

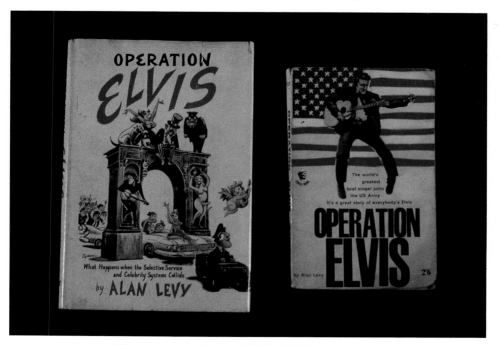

Illustration 148 — OPERATION ELVIS

Operation Elvis was authored by Alan Levy. The illustration on the left shows the first U.S. edition of **Operation Elvis** published in 1960. On the right is the paperback version of **Operation Elvis** published in England by Consul Books in 1962.

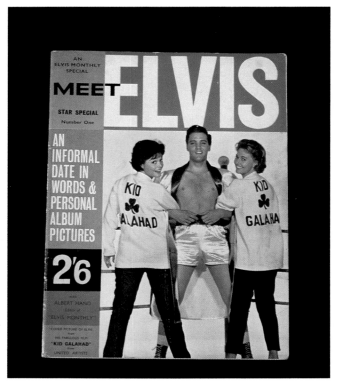

Illustration 149 — "MEET ELVIS" ANNUAL

Illustration 150 — COLLAGE OF ANNUALS
SALUTE TO ALBERT HAND

This page is dedicated to the late Albert Hand from England, who was responsible for the wonderful publications illustrated. "Meet Elvis" was the first special annual issued in 1962 with a softbound cover. The collage features the first hardbound annual issued in 1963, followed by yearly specials spanning the remainder of the '60s decade. Although published abroad, these publications became very popular among Elvis fans in the United States.

Illustration 151 — LIBERTY BOWL PROGRAM
This beautiful color picture graced the cover of the 1977 Liberty Bowl Football program featuring North Carolina versus Nebraska. This is the only item in the **Best of Elvis Collectibles** pertaining to Elvis after his death.

Popular magazines of the '60s and '70s, worth $12.00-$20.00.

NOVELTIES

**Illustration 152 —
ELVIS COIN PURSE**

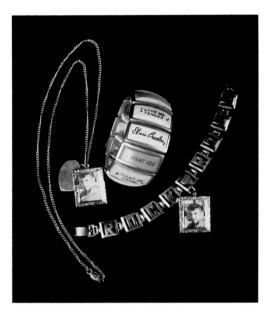

**Illustration 153 —
ELVIS JEWELRY**

**Illustration 154 —
ELVIS ZIPPER SCHOOL BINDER**

The items on this page are rare and quite unique. The manufacturers and copyrights, however, are unknown.

Illustration 155 — ELVIS FABRIC

Illustration 156 — ELVIS TEE SHIRT

Elvis' likeness has been used on both items featured in above illustrations. Once again, however, the manufacturer and copyright dates are unknown.

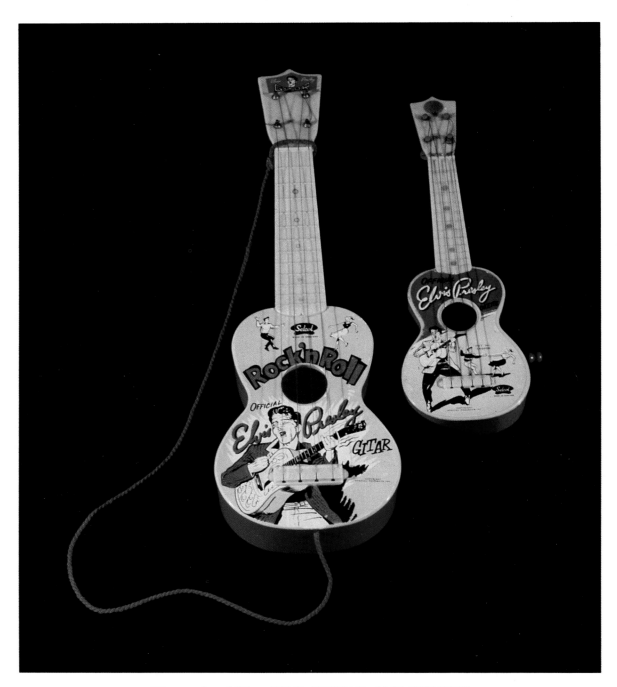

Illustration 157 — TOY GUITAR AND UKETTE
Both the guitar and ukette were manufactured by Selcol and made in England. These items are copyrighted by Special Projects Inc. Although neither one carried a copyright date, it is believed they were both manufactured in 1956 and are considered very rare.

ADVERTISEMENTS

AD RELATED SECTION

ADS

Collecting newspaper or magazine ads that advertised Elvis' movies, records, mail order photos, or 1956 Elvis Presley Enterprises products can be fun and basically inexpensive. The prices usually run at . . .

$8-$10 each — full page ads
$3-$5 each — half page ads
$1-$3 each — quarter page ads

They can be framed or just put into plastic pages to create your own scrapbook or reference file. Store posters (such as those advertising a product) or an in-store counter display (say from RCA record company) will, however, command a higher price. They are rare because they were not issued to sell to the customer. They were issued solely for advertising purposes.

The highest prices in the ad category would be for movie-related items, such as movie posters, inserts, banners, lobby cards, stills and press books.

HATCH SHOW PRINT
This poster, though incomplete, represents the first printer's run of blue. A second run of red, printing Elvis' name and date of show, would have followed.

FAN CLUB
Pink and Black — Fan Club Letter
Pink and Black — Membership Card
Pink and Black — Button

The headquarters for the first Elvis Presley National Fan Club was located in Madison, Tennessee. It is important to note that at a fan's request to join the Elvis Presley National Fan Club in early 1956, the member received more than the items pictured. These three items were accompanied by an 8″×10″ black and white photo that matched the three pictured items along with a tour photo album, "Mr. Dynamite".

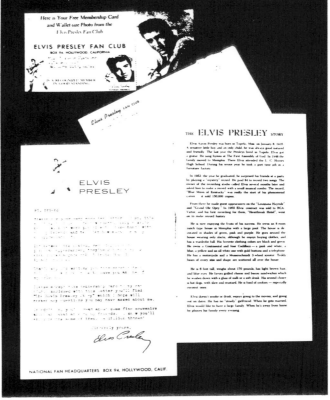

FAN CLUB

The headquarters for the Elvis Presley National Fan Club was moved from Madison, Tennessee, to Hollywood, California, later in 1956. It is believed the move took place during or after the filming of Elvis' first motion picture, "Love Me Tender".

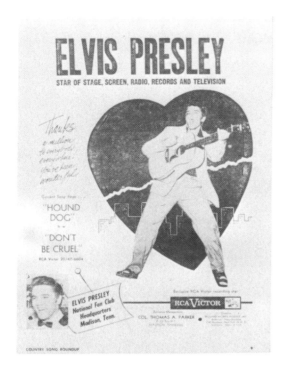

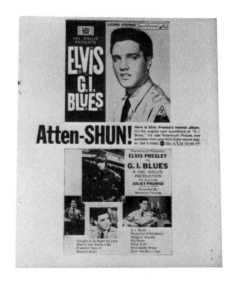

MAGAZINE ADVERTISEMENTS
PROMOTING ELVIS PRESLEY

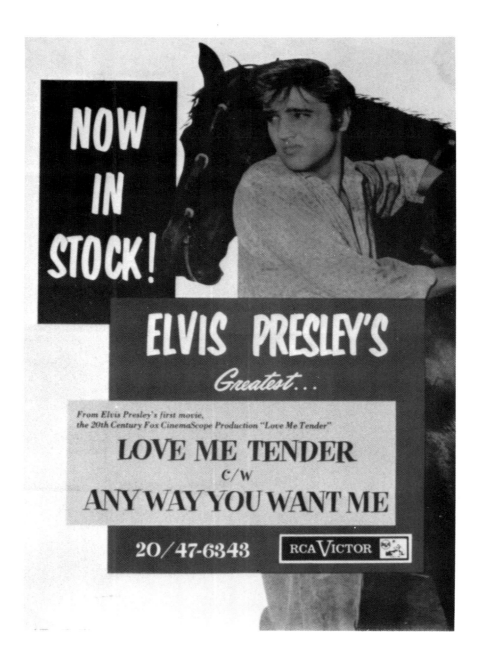

1956 STORE ADVERTISEMENT

This poster was used by stores to advertise Elvis' new 45 single ''Love Me Tender / Any Way You Want Me''. Poster measures 10″×14″.

CHARITY SHOW ADVERTISEMENT
This full page ad ran in the *Memphis Commercial Appeal* to inform the public of two charity shows Elvis gave in February of 1961 at the Ellis Auditorium in Memphis, Tennessee.

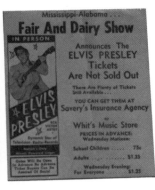

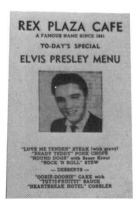

MISSISSIPPI-ALABAMA FAIR CONCERT

At 3:00 p.m. on September 26, 1956, one of the most famous concerts in history took place on the fairgrounds of the Mississippi-Alabama Fair. Illustrated above are many of the advertisements which celebrated Elvis' homecoming. Also included in the above illustration is a newspaper article from the *Memphis Commercial Appeal* newspaper capturing the special events from the day before.

STORE AND MAGAZINE ADVERTISEMENTS

The advertisements illustrated above were used either in stores or magazines to promote Elvis merchandise.

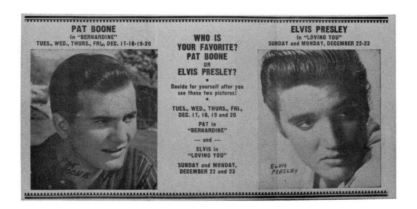

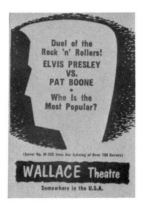

THEATRE FLYERS

Theatre flyers were used primarily by drive-in theatres and given to customers as they entered the theatre in order to inform them of the upcoming attractions.

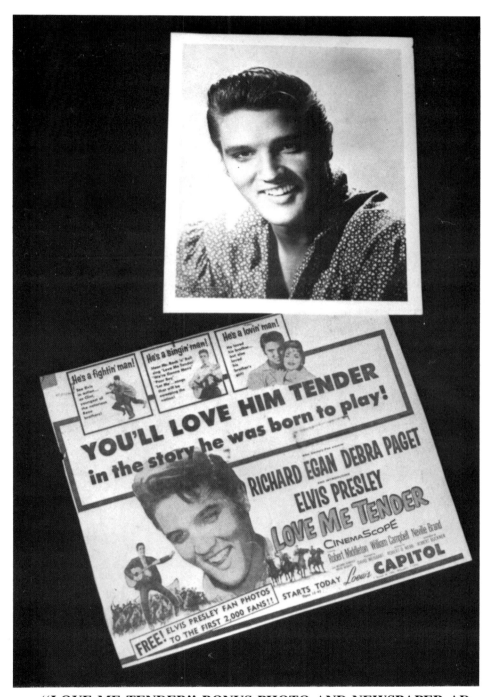

"LOVE ME TENDER" BONUS PHOTO AND NEWSPAPER AD

When the movie "Love Me Tender" opened in November 1956, the newspaper ads read, "FREE! ELVIS PRESLEY FAN PHOTOS TO THE FIRST 2000 FANS!!" Pictured here is one of those newspaper ads and the 8″×10″ black and white photo of Elvis as he appeared in the film.

BIG  D

JUNE 18, 1955

Official Program

10 cents

The Southwest's Biggest, Oldest, Boldest and Best Country Musical Attraction.

JAMBOREE

CHARLIE STREIGHT

Starring Tonight

ELVIS PRESLEY

"SCOTTY

&

BILL"

And All of the Jamboree Gang

**BROADCAST ON KRLD EVERY SATURDAY NIGHT 8:30 TO MIDNIGHT
CBS SATURDAY NIGHT COUNTRY STYLE — COAST-TO-COAST**

Look for Your Lucky Number!

Sportatorium

Ed McLemore
Producer

BIG "D" JAMBOREE

On Saturday, June 18, 1955, Elvis Presley appeared at the Big "D" Jamboree in Dallas, Texas.
This is the official program that sold for 10 cents that Saturday night. The back of the program had Elvis' picture and an article about the 20-year-old "fireball".
Elvis appeared from 8:00 to 8:30 p.m. to open the show and again from 9:00 to 9:30 p.m. The country stars also appearing that night included Sonny James and Johnny Hicks.

VALUE GUIDE

The value guide is to be used as a source of referral for Elvis collectors in their purchasing or selling of Elvis items.

The pricing is as accurate as possible, but — as collectors know — what an item will actually sell for depends on its condition, buyer enthusiasm, personal preference, scarcity, etc. The prices are meant as general guides and reflect prices at mail auctions, magazines, conventions, and by other serious collectors. It must be emphasized that the prices indicated in the book relate to pieces in excellent to mint condition. Actual purchase price should depend on the condition of the item. Items in less than mint condition should cost proportionately less. Some items are so rare, however, that even in poor condition, they will still bring a small percentage of their mint value.

Items protected by copyright and patent laws are described and illustrated in this book for educational purposes only, as permitted by these laws, to enable readers to identify and evaluate original Elvis Presley memorabilia.

The author reminds readers that these descriptions and illustrations are to be used for no other purposes.

ELVIS PRESLEY ENTERPRISES

Illustration #	Item	Value
1)	1956 EPE Bookend (single)	$400.00
2)	1956 EPE Zipper School Binder	$1,025.00
3)	Item A - 1956 EPE Pencils (pack)	$220.00
	Item B - Shipping Box for Pencils	$130.00
	Item C - Pre-price Tag for Pencils	$50.00
4)	1956 EPE Zipper School Binder	$1,025.00
5)	1956 EPE "Mr. Teenager"	$1,000.00
6A)	EPE Pictures with Molded Frames	$330.00
6B)	Item A - 1956 EPE Photo Album	$515.00
	Item B - 1956 EPE Autograph Book	$520.00
	Item C - 1956 EPE Scrapbook	$500.00
	Item D - 1956 EPE Record Case	$575.00
	Item E - 1956 EPE Diary	$560.00
7)	1956 EPE Wallet Display Card	$375.00
8)	1956 EPE Plastic Belts	$500.00
9)	Item A - EPE Billfold	$485.00
	Item B - EPE Rock and Roll Billfold	$575.00
	Item C - EPE Photo Wallet	$480.00
	Item D - EPE French Purse	$600.00
10)	EPE French Purse (navy)	$600.00
11)	EPE Billfold	$485.00
12)	EPE Overnight Case	$650.00
13)	EPE Photo Wallet	$650.00
14)	EPE Carry All Bag	$725.00
15)	Guitar Pin	$220.00
16)	Item A - Pinback Buttons (each)	$75.00-$90.00
	Item B - Celluloid Pin	$100.00
17)	Label for Elvis Sideburns	$50.00
18)	1956 Pinback Buttons (each)	$40.00-$50.00
19)	Item A - Lipstick Chart	$200.00
	Item B - 1956 EPE Lipstick on Card	$670.00
20)	1957 EPE "Teddy Bear" Perfume	$250.00
21)	1956 EPE Scarf	$530.00
22)	Dog Tag Necklace in complete package	$330.00

Illustration #	Item	Value
23)	Item A - 1956 Sweater Holder	$290.00
	Item B - "Love Me Tender" Necklace	$300.00
	Item C - 1956 Key Chain	$160.00
24)	Item A - Charm Bracelet (Canada - Blue)	$135.00
	Item B - Charm Bracelet (USA - Red)	$220.00
25)	Item A - 1956 Earrings	$425.00
	Item B - 1956 Guitar Pin	$550.00
	Item C - 1956 Photo Charm Bracelet	$600.00
26)	1956 EPE Aluminum Medallion	$220.00
27)	1956 EPE Rings on Card (complete)	$2,000.00
	Item A - 1956 EPE Ring	$160.00
	Item B - 1956 Display Card	$375.00
28)	1956 EPE Ashtray (or) Coaster	$340.00
29)	Item A - 1956 EPE Drinking Glass	$225.00
	Item B - 1956 EPE Glass Plate	$575.00
30)	1956 EPE "Love Me Tender" Pillow	$365.00
31)	1956 EPE Throw Pillow	$435.00
32)	1956 EPE Handkerchiefs	$460.00
33)	1956 EPE Handkerchief	$460.00
34)	1956 EPE Mittens	$820.00
35)	1956 EPE Tee Shirt	$440.00
36)	1956 EPE Leather Belt	$565.00
37)	1956 EPE Blue Jeans Tag	$125.00
38)	Item A - 1956 Crew Hat	$110.00
	Item B - 1956 Pinback Buttons (each)	$25.00
39)	1956 EPE Boatneck Shirt	$475.00
40)	1956 EPE Felt Skirt	$1,125.00
41)	Item A - Box for Pump Shoes	$450.00
	Item B - 1956 EPE Pump Shoes	$950.00
42)	1956 EPE Sneakers in the Box	$1,350.00
	Item A - 1956 EPE Sneakers	$860.00
	Item B - Box for Sneakers	$470.00
43)	1956 EPE Statuette	$650.00
44)	1957 EPE Doll in the Box	$2,300.00
	Item A - 1957 EPE Doll	$1,800.00
	Item B - Box for Doll	$200.00

Illustration #	Item	Value
45)	- 1957 Paint by Number Set (complete)	$1,800.00
46)	- Item A - 1956 Bubble Gum Box	$900.00
	Item B - 1956 1 cent Gum Wrapper	$100.00
	Item C - 1956 5 cent Gum Wrapper	$165.00
47)	- 1956 EPE Bubble Gum Cards	$600.00
48)	- 1956 EPE Guitar and Carrying Case	$1,700.00
	Item A - 1956 EPE Guitar	$1,000.00
49)	- 1957 EPE Game	$1,350.00
50)	- 1961 EPE Gold Bust	$600.00
51)	- 1957 EPE Promotional Photo	$60.00
52)	- 1957 EPE John's Pocket Movie	$75.00
53)	- Item A - 1956 Photo in Molded Frame	$330.00
	Item B - 1956 Hot Plate	$330.00
	Item C - Celluloid Pin	$25.00
	Item D - Celluloid Pin	$25.00

RCA & SUN

54)	- Item A - 4-speed Model Record Player	$1,000.00
	Item B - Automatic 45 Record Player	$1,150.00
	Item C - Instructions for Record Player	$100.00
55)	- Bonus Photo	
	Item A - 1963 Calendar "Girls, Girls, Girls"	
	with Christmas Message	$250.00
	singles on back	$90.00
	albums on back	$80.00
	Item B - "World's Fair"	$150.00
	Item C - "Elvis Sings Burning Love"	$50.00
	Item D - "Elvis Golden Records Vol. 4"	$175.00
56)	- "King Creole" Bonus Photo	$150.00
57)	- 1963 Pocket Calendar	$60.00
57A)	- Set of Original Pocket Calendars	$150.00
58)	- Christmas Card	
	Item A - 1975	$20.00
	Item B - 1958	$100.00
	Item C - 1967	$15.00
	Item D - 1974	$20.00
	Item E - 1960	$50.00
	Item F - 1959 w/message	$50.00
	Item F - 1959 w/o message	$40.00
	Item G - 1961	$40.00
	Item H - 1966	$40.00
	Item I - 1971	$20.00
	Item J - 1963	$50.00
	Item K - 1968	$25.00
	Item L - 1972	$20.00
59)	- 1968 Singer TV Special Catalog	$60.00
60)	- 1956 Concert Ticket (complete)	$150.00
61)	- 1959 Record Catalog	$60.00
62)	- "Aloha from Hawaii" Concert Ticket	$200.00
63)	- RCA Christmas Poster 1967	$150.00
64)	- 1967 Christmas Catalog	$60.00
65)	- Elvis Publicity Photo (SUN)	$250.00
66)	- Five SUNs complete as illustrated	$2,000.00
67)	- Item A - RCA EPB-1254 Sleeve	$1,000.00

Illustration #	Item	Value
	Item B - RCA EPA-747 Sleeve	$2,000.00
	Item C - "This is His Life" Sleeve	$1,500.00

SHEET MUSIC & PHOTOGRAPHS

68)	- Item A - "Stuck on You"	$40.00
	Item B - "Too Much"	$50.00
	Item C - "All Shook Up"	$35.00
	Item D - "Heartbreak Hotel"	$30.00
	Item E - "One Night"	$40.00
	Item F - "Ready Teddy"	$50.00
	Item G - "Don't Be Cruel"	$35.00
	Item H - "When Your Heartache Begins"	$35.00
	Item I - "Blue Hawaii"	$50.00
69)	- "Old Shep"	$125.00
70)	- "I Don't Care if the Sun Don't Shine"	$100.00
71)	- "Elvis Presley for President"	$100.00
72)	- "Burning Love"	$15.00
73)	- Item A - 4"×5" 1956 Photographs	$60.00
	Item B - 8"×10" 1956 Photographs	$40.00
74)	- Pastel Photographs 8"×10" (group)	$20.00

LAS VEGAS & CONCERTS

75)	- Collage	$250.00
76)	- 1955 Concert Poster	$250.00
77)	- Item A - "Mr. Dynamite"	$275.00
	Item B - "Mr. Rhythm"	$350.00
	Item C - "Photo Folio"	$175.00
78)	- 1956 EPE Souvenir Photo Album	$175.00
79)	- Menu 1969 International Hotel	$250.00
80)	- Item A - Menu 1971 Sahara Tahoe Hotel	$75.00
	Item B - Menu 1973 Sahara Tahoe Hotel	$75.00
81)	- Menu 1975 Las Vegas Hilton	$75.00
82)	- Elvis Concert Pennants	$40.00
83)	- Item A - Hound Dog - Souvenir	$125.00
	Item B - Summer Festival Pennant	$75.00
	Item C - Summer Festival Straw Hat	$75.00
84)	- Oil Cloth Banner	$275.00
85)	- 1969 International Hotel Poster	$150.00

MOVIES

86)	- Movie Collage	
	Item "Love Me Tender" Insert Poster	$300.00
87)	- "Love Me Tender" Banner	$800.00
88)	- "Loving You" Banner	$800.00
89)	- "Jailhouse Rock" Banner	$1,000.00
90)	- "Love Me Tender" Pressbook	$200.00
91)	- "Loving You" Pressbook	$150.00
92)	- "Jailhouse Rock" Pressbook	$125.00
93)	- "King Creole" Pressbook	$125.00
94)	- "Love Me Tender" 30"×40" Poster	$800.00
95)	- Theatre Pictorial	$250.00
96)	- "Love Me Tender" Lobby Cards (set)	$850.00
97)	- "Loving You" Window Card	$200.00
98)	- "Loving You" Lobby Photo Poster	$200.00

Illustration #	Item	Value
99) -	"Loving You" One Sheet Poster	$325.00
100) -	"Loving You" Lobby Cards (original)	$650.00
101) -	"Loving You" Lobby Cards (reissue)	$650.00
102) -	"Jailhouse Rock" Insert Poster	$275.00
103) -	"Jailhouse Rock" Lobby Cards	$800.00
104) -	"Jailhouse Rock" Window Card	$200.00
105) -	"King Creole" original Lobby Poster	$225.00
106) -	"King Creole" reissue Lobby Poster	$225.00
107) -	"King Creole" original Lobby Cards	$450.00
108) -	"King Creole" reissue Lobby Cards	$500.00
109) -	"G.I. Blues" One Sheet Poster	$200.00
110) -	"G.I. Blues" Lobby Cards (set)	$225.00
111) -	"Blue Hawaii" One Sheet Poster	$200.00
112) -	"Blue Hawaii" Lobby Cards (set)	$240.00
113) -	"G.I. Blues" Hat	$75.00
114) -	"Blue Hawaii" Lei Medallion	$150.00
115) -	"Jailhouse Rock" Pressbook Herald	$45.00
116) -	"Love Me Tender" Standee	$1,000.00
117) -	"Loving You" Standee	$900.00
118) -	"Jailhouse Rock" Movie Prop	$2,000.00

PUBLICATIONS

Illustration #	Item	Value
119) -	Item A - *Rock and Roll Review*, Dec. 1956	$60.00
	Item B - *Rock and Roll Review*, Oct. 1956	$60.00
	Item C - *COOL*, April 1957	$75.00
	Item D - *Rock 'N Roll Stars #2*, 1957	$55.00
	Item E - *Rock 'N Roll Stars #1*, 1956	$65.00
	Item F - *Teen Life*, April 1957	$65.00
	Item G - *16 Magazine*, May 1957	$55.00
120) -	Comic "Young Lovers" 1957	$185.00
121) -	*Elvis in the Army* 1959	$70.00
122) -	Item A - *Roanoke Times Parade*, June 1960	$60.00
	Item B - *Sunday Mirror*	$30.00
	Item C - *Roanoke Times Parade*, Nov. 1962	$25.00
	Item D - *Roanoke Times Parade*, Mar. 1962	$25.00
	Item E - *New York News Coloroto*	$25.00
	Item F - *Detroit Free Press Parade*	$35.00
123) -	*New York Sunday Mirror*, Feb. 1957	$35.00
124) -	Item A - *Hep Cats*, Dec. 1957	$75.00
	Item B - *Hep Cats*, Feb. 1956	$75.00
	Item C - *Cool and Hep Cats*, 1958	$75.00
125) -	Item A - *DIG*, Nov. 1956	$75.00
	Item B - *DIG*, Jan. 1957	$75.00
	Item C - *DIG*, May 1958	$75.00
126) -	*True Strange*, June 1957	$75.00
127) -	*Rock and Roll Roundup*, April 1957	$100.00
128) -	*Modern Teen*, August 1957	$60.00
129) -	*Teen*, June 1958	$100.00
130) -	*Pose!*, April 1957	$100.00
131) -	Item A - *Elvis Answers Back* (speaks)	$225.00
	Item B - *Elvis Answers Back* (truth)	$225.00

Illustration #	Item	Value
132) -	Item A - *TV Star Parade*, 1956	$40.00
	Item B - *Elvis and Jimmy*, 1956	$100.00
	Item C - *Rock and Roll Rivals #1*, 1957	$50.00
	Item D - *16 Magazine*, July 1957	$45.00
	Item E - *Rock 'N Roll Battler*, 1956	$60.00
	Item F - *Elvis vs. The Beatles*, 1965	$85.00
133) -	Item A - *Elvis Presley - Hero or Heel*	$135.00
	Item B - *Elvis Presley*, 1956	$85.00
	Item C - *The Amazing Elvis Presley*, 1956	$90.00
	Item D - *Elvis Photo Album*, 1956	$85.00
	Item E - *Elvis Presley Speaks*, 1956	$85.00
	Item F - Official *Elvis Presley Album*	$85.00
	Item G - *Elvis - The Intimate Story*, 1956	$100.00
134) -	*TV Radio Mirror*, December 1956	$50.00
135) -	*The Enthusiast*, May 1956	$100.00
136) -	*The Cash Box*, March 18, 1961	$50.00
137) -	*Country Song Roundup*, February 1957	$45.00
138) -	*Cowboy Songs #48*, 1956	$65.00
139) -	*Hollywood Rebels*, 1957	$50.00
140) -	*Films and Filming*, August 1966	$45.00
141) -	*Stardom*, September 1959	$30.00
142) -	*Elvis in Hollywood*, 1956	$100.00
143) -	*New York Sunday News Coloroto*, 1956	$40.00
144) -	Item A - *TV Guide*, Sept. 8-14, 1956	$125.00
	Item B - *TV Guide*, May 7-13, 1960	$75.00
145) -	*Chicago Tribune TV Week*, July 7-13, 1956	$40.00
146) -	*Radio TV Life*, Nov. 24-30, 1956	$50.00
147) -	*The Elvis Presley Story*	$75.00
148) -	Item A - *Operation Elvis* (hardback)	$80.00
	Item B - *Operation Elvis* (paperback)	$55.00
149) -	"Meet Elvis" 1962 Annual	$100.00
150) -	Item A - 1963 Elvis Annual	$60.00
	Item B - 1964 Elvis Annual	$35.00
	Item C - 1965 Elvis Annual	$35.00
	Item D - 1966 Elvis Annual	$35.00
	Item E - 1967 Elvis Annual	$35.00
	Item F - 1968 Elvis Annual	$35.00
	Item G - 1969 Elvis Annual	$25.00
151) -	Liberty Bowl Program	$75.00

NOVELTIES

Illustration #	Item	Value
152) -	Elvis Coin Purse	$175.00
153) -	Item A - Rock 'N Roll Bracelet	$150.00
	Item B - Elvis Presley Bracelet	$150.00
	Item C - Rock 'N Roll Necklace	$150.00
154) -	Zipper School Binder	$350.00
155) -	Fabric	$150.00
156) -	Elvis Tee Shirt	$100.00
157) -	Item A - Toy Guitar	$1,000.00
	Item B - Toy Ukette	$1,000.00